THE HOUSE OF BELONGING

THE
HOUSE
of
BELONGING

Poems by DAVID WHYTE

2 0  0 2

MANY RIVERS PRESS

LANGLEY, WASHINGTON

*This book is dedicated to Brendan Whyte
and the house he will make
from his own belonging.*

COPYRIGHT © 1997 DAVID WHYTE
ISBN 0-9621524-3-9

1st Printing: 1997
2nd Printing: 1997
3rd Printing: 1998
4th Printing: 1999
5th Printing: 2002

LOST

Stand still. The trees ahead and bushes beside you
Are not lost. Wherever you are is called Here,
And you must treat it as a powerful stranger,
Must ask permission to know it and be known.
The forest breathes. Listen. It answers,
I have made this place around you.
If you leave it, you may come back again, saying Here.
No two trees are the same to Raven.
No two branches are the same to Wren.
If what a tree or a bush does is lost on you,
You are surely lost. Stand still. The forest knows
Where you are. You must let it find you.

David Wagoner
copyright 1976

CONTENTS

CONTENTS *(continued)*

IV. BELONGING TO THOSE I KNOW

[I]

BELONGING TO THE HOUSE

THIS LIFE

At the center of this life
there is a man I want to know again.
He has a new house,
a clear view of the mountain
and hidden in the close grained wood
of his desk
a new book of poems.

He has left the life
he once tried to love
now it is only a shadow
calling for another shadow

and this shadow
wants to become real again

it falls against walls
and fences
and stairways

the dark penumbra of my belonging

now let me cast my shadow
against life

before the specter haunts me to my
grave.

THE HOUSE OF BELONGING

I awoke
this morning
in the gold light
turning this way
and that

thinking for
a moment
it was one
day
like any other.

But
the veil had gone
from my
darkened heart
and
I thought

it must have been the quiet
candlelight
that filled my room,

it must have been
the first
easy rhythm
with which I breathed
myself to sleep,

it must have been
the prayer I said
speaking to the otherness
of the night.

And
I thought
this is the good day
you could
meet your love,

this is the black day
someone close
to you could die.

This is the day
you realize
how easily the thread
is broken
between this world
and the next

and I found myself
sitting up
in the quiet pathway
of light,

the tawny
close grained cedar
burning round
me like fire
and all the angels of this housely
heaven ascending
through the first
roof of light
the sun has made.

This is the bright home
in which I live,
this is where
I ask
my friends
to come,
this is where I want
to love all the things
it has taken me so long
to learn to love.

This is the temple
of my adult aloneness
and I belong
to that aloneness
as I belong to my life.

There is no house
like the house of belonging.

AT HOME

At home amidst
the bees
wandering
the garden
in the summer
light
the sky
a broad roof
for the house
of contentment
where I wish
to
live forever
in the eternity
of my own
fleeting
and momentary
happiness.

I walk toward
the kitchen
door as if walking
toward the
door of a recognized
heaven

and see the
simplicity
of shelves and
the blue dishes
and the
vaporing

steam rising
from the kettle
that called me in.

Not just this
aromatic cup
from which to drink
but the flavor
of a life made whole
and lovely
through the
imagination
seeking its way.

Not just this
house around me
but the arms
of a fierce
but healing world.

Not just this line
I write
but the
innocence
of an earned
forgiveness
flowing again
through hands
made new with
writing.

And a man
with no company
but his house,
his garden,
and his own
well peopled solitude,

entering
the silences
and chambers
of the heart
to start again.

IT HAPPENS TO THOSE WHO LIVE ALONE

It happens to those
who live alone
that they feel sure
of visitors
when no one else
is there,

until the one day
and one particular
hour
working in the
quiet garden,

when the
green bud
at the center
of their slowly
opening silence
flowers
in belonging

and they realize
at once,
that all along
they have been
an invitation
to everything
and every kind of trouble

and that life
happens by
to those who
inhabit
silence

like the bees
visiting
the tall mallow
on their legs of gold,
or the wasps
going from door to door
in the tall forest
of the daisies.

I have my freedom
today
because
nothing really happened

and nobody came
to see me.
Only the slow
growing of the garden
in the summer heat

and the silence of that
unborn life
making itself
known at my desk,

my hands
still
dark with the
crumbling soil
as I write
and watch

the first lines
of a new poem,
like flowers
of scarlet fire,
coming to fullness
in a new light.

WINTER CHILD

Myself at my door
like Blake
at home in his
heaven
my own heart
newly opened
by the news
and my face
turned upward
and innocent
toward them.

All the stars
like a great crowd
of creation singing

above the blessed house.

WHAT I MUST TELL MYSELF

Above the water
and against the mountain
the geese fly through the
brushed darkness
of the early morning
and out into the light,

they travel over
my immovable house
with such unison
of faith
and with such
assurance
toward the south

cresting the mountains
and the long
coast of a continent

as they move
each year
toward a horizon
they have learned
to call their own.

I know this house,
and this horizon,
and this world I have made.
I know this silence
and the particular treasures
and terrors
of this belonging
but I cannot know the world
to which I am going.

I have only this breath
and this presence
for my wings
and they carry me
in my body
whatever I do
from one hushed moment
to another.

I know my innocence
and I know my unknowing
but for all my successes
I go through life
like a blind child
who cannot see,
arms outstretched
trying to put together
a world.

And the world
works on my behalf
catching me in its arms
when I go too far.

I don't know what
I could have done
to have earned such faith.

But what of all the others
and the bitter lovers
and the ones who were not held?

Life turns like a slow river
and suddenly you are there
at the edge of the water
with all the rest
and the fire carries the
feast and the laughter
and in the darkness
away from the fire
the unspoken griefs
that still
make togetherness
but then

just as suddenly
it has become a fireless
friendless
night again
and you find yourself alone
and you must speak to the stars
or the rain-filled clouds
or anything at hand
to find your place.

When you are alone
you must do anything
to believe
and when you are
abandoned
you must speak
with everything
you know
and everything you are
in order
to belong.

If I have no one to turn to
I must claim my aloneness.

If I cannot speak
I must reclaim the prison
of my body.

If I have only darkness
I must claim the night.

And then,
even in the closest dark
the world
can find me

and if I have honor
enough
for the place in which it finds me
I will know
it is speaking to me
and where I must go.

Watching the geese
go south I find
that
even in silence
and even in stillness
and
even in my home
alone
without a thought
or a movement
I am part
of a great migration
that will take me to another place.

And though all the things I love
may pass away and
the great family of things and people
I have made around me
will see me go,
I feel them living in me
like a great gathering
ready to reach a greater home.

When one thing dies all things
die together, and must live again
in a different way,
when one thing
is missing everything is missing,
and must be found again
in a new whole
and everything wants to be complete,
everything wants to go home
and the geese travelling south
are like the shadow of my breath
flying into the darkness
on great heart-beats
to an unknown land where I belong.

This morning they have
found me,
full of faith,
like a blind child,
nestled in their feathers,
following the great coast of the wind
to a home I cannot see.

[II]

BELONGING TO THE NIGHT

SWEET DARKNESS

When your eyes are tired
the world is tired also.

When your vision has gone
no part of the world can find you.

Time to go into the dark
where the night has eyes
to recognize its own.

There you can be sure
you are not beyond love.

The dark will be your womb
tonight.

The night will give you a horizon
further than you can see.

You must learn one thing.
The world was made to be free in.

Give up all the other worlds
except the one to which you belong.

Sometimes it takes darkness and the sweet
confinement of your aloneness
to learn

anything or anyone
that does not bring you alive

is too small for you.

ALL THE TRUE VOWS

All the true vows
are secret vows
the ones we speak out loud
are the ones we break.

There is only one life
you can call your own
and a thousand others
you can call by any name you want.

Hold to the truth you make
every day with your own body,
don't turn your face away.

Hold to your own truth
at the center of the image
you were born with.

Those who do not understand
their destiny will never understand
the friends they have made
nor the work they have chosen

nor the one life that waits
beyond all the others.

By the lake in the wood
in the shadows
you can
whisper that truth
to the quiet reflection
you see in the water.

Whatever you hear from
the water, remember,

it wants you to carry
the sound of its truth on your lips.

Remember,
in this place
no one can hear you

and out of the silence
you can make a promise
it will kill you to break,

that way you'll find
what is real and what is not.

I know what I am saying.
Time almost forsook me
and I looked again.

Seeing my reflection
I broke a promise
and spoke
for the first time
after all these years

in my own voice,

before it was too late
to turn my face again.

WHAT TO REMEMBER WHEN WAKING

In that first
hardly noticed
moment
in which you wake,
coming back
to this life
from the other
more secret,
moveable
and frighteningly
honest
world
where everything
began,
there is a small
opening
into the day
which closes
the moment
you begin
your plans.

What you can plan
is too small
for you to live.

What you can live
wholeheartedly
will make plans
enough
for the vitality
hidden in your sleep.

To be human
is to become visible
while carrying
what is hidden
as a gift to others.

To remember
the other world
in this world
is to live in your
true inheritance.

You are not
a troubled guest
on this earth,
you are not
an accident
amidst other accidents
you were invited
from another and greater
night
than the one
from which
you have just emerged.

Now, looking through
the slanting light
of the morning
window toward
the mountain
presence

of everything
that can be,
what urgency
calls you to your
one love? What shape
waits in the seed
of you to grow
and spread
its branches
against a future sky?

Is it waiting
in the fertile sea?
In the trees
beyond the house?
In the life
you can imagine
for yourself?
In the open
and lovely
white page
on the waiting desk?

THE WINTER OF LISTENING

No one but me by the fire,
my hands burning
red in the palms while
the night wind carries
everything away outside.

All this petty worry
while the great cloak
of the sky grows dark
and intense
round every living thing.

What is precious
inside us does not
care to be known
by the mind
in ways that diminish
its presence.

What we strive for
in perfection
is not what turns us
into the lit angel
we desire,

what disturbs
and then nourishes
has everything
we need.

What we hate
in ourselves
is what we cannot know
in ourselves but
what is true to the pattern
does not need
to be explained.

Inside everyone
is a great shout of joy
waiting to be born.

Even with summer
so far off
I feel it grown in me
now and ready
to arrive in the world.

All those years
listening to those
who had
nothing to say.

All those years
forgetting
how everything
has its own voice
to make
itself heard.

All those years
forgetting
how easily
you can belong
to everything
simply by listening.

And the slow
difficulty
of remembering
how everything
is born from
an opposite
and miraculous
otherness.

Silence and winter
has lead me to that
otherness.

So let this winter
of listening
be enough
for the new life
I must call my own.

Every sound
has a home
from which it has come
to us
and a door
through which it is going
again
out into the world
to make another home.

We speak
only with the voices
of those
we can hear ourselves
and the body has a voice
only for that portion
of the body of the world
it has learned to perceive.

It becomes
a world itself
by listening
hard
for the way
it belongs.

There it can
learn
how it
must be
and what
it must do.

And
here
in the tumult
of the night
I hear the walnut
above the child's swing
swaying
its dark limbs
in the wind
and the rain now
come to
beat against my window
and somewhere
in this cold night
of wind and stars
the first whispered
opening of
those hidden
and invisible springs
that uncoil
in the still summer air
each yet
to be imagined
rose.

THE WELL OF STARS

Blue lights on the runway like stars
on the surface of a well
into which I fall each night from the sky,
emerging through the tunnel door
of the jetway, and the black waters
of the night, in the cities of America.

In the lit rooms of glass and steel,
in the still and secret towers,
under the true stars hid by cloud
and the steam shrouded roofs
of the mansions of money and hope,
I come with my quiet voice and
my insistence, and my stories,
and out of that second and
deeper well I see again those other
blue stars and that other darkness
closer even than the night outside,
the one we refuse to mention,
the darkness we know so well
inside everyone.

I have a few griefs and joys
I can call my own
and through accident it seems,
a steadfast faith in each of them
and that's what I will say
matters when the story ends.

But it takes a little while to get there,
all the unburdening
and the laying down
and the willingness
to really tire of yourself,
and then step by step
the ways
the poets through time
generously gave themselves
to us,
walking like pilgrims
through doubt,
combining their fear
their fierceness and their faith.

And you now,
in the front of the room
under the florescent light
by the reflected window
hiding all the stars
you have forgotten.

One more member
of the prison population
whose eyes have caught
the open gate at last.
You are the one for whom the gift was made.

Keep that look in your eyes
and you'll gladly grow tired of your reflection.

All this way through
the great cloud race between
here and Seattle, just
to look beneath your face.

There, for all to see,
the well of stars,
and the great night from which you were born.

THE JOURNEY

Above the mountains
the geese turn into
the light again

painting their
black silhouettes
on an open sky.

Sometimes everything
has to be
enscribed across
the heavens

so you can find
the one line
already written
inside you.

Sometimes it takes
a great sky
to find that

first, bright
and indescribable
wedge of freedom
in your own heart.

Sometimes with
 the bones of the black
  sticks left when the fire
   has gone out

someone has written
 something new
  in the ashes
   of your life.

*You are not leaving
 you are arriving.*

[III]

BELONGING TO PLACES

YORKSHIRE

I love the dead
and their quiet living
underground
and I love the rain
on my face.

And in childhood
I loved the wind
on the moors
that carried the rain
and that carried the ashes
of the dead
like a spring sowing
of memory
stored through all
the winters past.

In the dark November
onset of the winter
in which I was born,
I was set down in the
folds of that land
as if I belonged there,
and in that first night
under the evening shadow
of the moors and most likely
with the wind in the west,
as it would be for most
of my growing life

I was breathing in the tang
and troubles of that immense
and shadowing sky
as I was breathing the shadows
of my mother's body,
learning who and what was close
and how I could belong.

What great and
abstract power
lent me to those
particularities
I cannot know
but body
and soul were made
for that belonging.

Yorkshire is as hard
as a spade-edge
but the underpinnings
of the people and the land
in which we lived
flowed and turned like the
river I knew in my valley.
The blunt solidity of my elders
floated like mountains
on the slow but fluid lava
of their history.

But on this solid yet floating
land I must have been
as Irish as my mother
and amid the straight certainties
of my father's Yorkshire
I felt beneath the damp moor's
horizon the curved invisible
lines that drew everything
together, the underground stream
of experience that could not
be quarried or brought to the surface
but only dowsed, felt, followed
or intuited from above.

Poetry then became the key, my way
underground into what was hidden
by the inept but daily coverings
of grown-up surface speech.
Something sacred in the land
was left unsaid in people's mouths
but was written into our inheritance
and that small volume of Thom Gunn's
youthful poetry from
the library's high tiptoe shelf
was the angel's gift to me.
Opened and read in my
young boy's hands
it revealed the first code
I sought and needed to begin
speaking what I felt
had been forgotten.

Full stretch I reached again
along the spines and touched
another *other* life, pulling
down into my hands
The Hawk in the Rain.
Ted Hughes' dark book full of northern omens
hovering above my
own child's shadow on the ground,
my heart and mind
caught in those written claws
and whisked into the sky.
The first rush of poetry's
extended arms a complete
abduction of my person.

That was the beginning.
The first line on the open page
of my new life, the rest
would be more difficult
but that was the soil in which
I would grow, and that was the
life *into* which I would grow,
blessed and badgered by the northern
sweeps of light and dark
and the old entanglements
to which I was born. Always
on the wuthering moors
the gifts and stories and poetry
of the unknown and unvisited dead
who brought their history
to the world in which I grew.

Orphaned by poetry
from my first home
to find a greater home
out in the world
I wandered from that land
and began to write
youthfully and insubstantially,
slowly making myself
real and seeable by writing
myself into an original world
which had borne and
grown me so generously.

Belonging to one old land
so much by birth
I learn each day now
what it means to
be born into a new land
and new people. The open
moor of the American
mind gusted and shaken
by imagined new worlds
and imagined new clouds
and the fears and griefs of
the peopled and unknowable distances
of a vast land, and still amidst
everything, an innocence
which survives here untouched
amidst a difficult inheritance.

Let my history then
be a gate unfastened
to a new life
and not a barrier
to my becoming.
Let me find the ghosts
and histories and barely
imagined future
of this world,
and let me now have
the innocence to grow
just as well in shadow or light
by what is gifted
in this land
as the one to which I was born.

ELDERFLOWER

White amongst the deep green,
the midsummer air of memory
is round each blossom for me.

Their glimmering scented
innocence swirling
the quiet past to life.

So that rising above
the leaves and crowded faces
I see in the mind's eye
my mother's new elderflower
wine lifted to the light.

A pale and humble North
Country sherry that was
sappy and full in the mouth,
filling the chest with
cool green vowels
grown straight from that
familiar land
where first I walked,
then loved, then wrote.

Even in the forced
immediacy
of taste and memory,
speech is still speechless
to describe
the subtleties unmasked
by that quiet stream
on the
silenced tongue.

A clear, unspoken
and granted magic
drawn yearly
from the yeasting
bottle
in the pantry bottom.

On the lane to Hartshead
the elder trees
themselves
still live from year to year
like a bright
avenue of bridal posies
a continual celebration
of some other-worldly
marriage through which
I walk each year
on my return.

They flank my walk
through all the years
of memory
and all the summers
and fullness and
arrogant innocence
of that youthful
inheritance.

They live in me now
as they live in the world
growing and flowering
and then retreating

when I forget them
to a mere silhouette
in the chill winters
when I cannot
recall the June air
in Yorkshire.

But that scent from
the lifted glass
of my mother's
making
is a pure memory
of summer made new

and the old faces
round the table
welcome me back,
nodding and talking
to the music
of gathering,

my mother laughing
tipsily at our
repeated
congratulation
and time stopped

by the stirred plangency
of the blossom
in the wine,
that taste overwhelming
my present

and the bottle
passed round
once more and
handed back
down the years to me.

So far away now
but for the cool
sibilant taste
of what is
gifted to us

through time
flowering again
in the memory

moment to present moment.

TEN YEARS LATER

When the mind is clear
and the surface of the now still,
now swaying water

slaps against
the rolling kayak,

I find myself near darkness
paddling again to Yellow Island.

Every spring wildflowers
cover the grey rocks.

Every year the sea breeze
ruffles the cold and lovely pearls
hidden in the center of the flowers

as if remembering them
by touch alone.

A calm and lonely, trembling beauty
that frightened me in youth.

Now their loneliness
feels familiar, one small thing
I've learned these years,

how to be alone,
and at the edge of aloneness
how to be found by the world.

Innocence is what we allow
to be gifted back to us
once we've given ourselves away.

There is one world only,
the one to which we gave ourselves
utterly, and to which one day

we are blessed to return.

FOUR HORSES

On Thursday the farmer
put four horses
into the cut hay-field
next to the house.

Since then the days
have been filled with the
sheen of their
brown hides
racing the fence edge.

Since then I see
their curved necks
through the kitchen window
sailing like swans
past the pale field.

Each morning
their hooves fill my
open door
with an urgency
for something
just beyond my grasp

and I spend my whole
day in an idiot joy
writing, gardening,
and looking
for it
under every stone.

I find myself
wanting to do
something
stupid and lovely.

I find myself
wanting to walk up
and thank
the farmer for those
dark brown horses and
see him stand
back laughing in his
grizzled and
denim wonder at my
innocence.

I find myself wanting
to run down First Street
like an eight year old
saying, "Hey!
Come and look
at the new horses
in Fossek's field!"

And I find myself
wanting to ride
into the last hours
of this summer
bareback and
happy as the hooves
of the days
that drum toward me.

I hear the whinny of
their fenced and abandoned
freedom
and feel happy
today
in the field
of my own making,

writing non-stop,
my head held high,
ranging the boundaries
of a birthright
exuberance.

THE HORSE WHISPERER

Ireland's the ghost-horse
all right,
rearing out of history
like the wraith-herd seen
at Fanore.

After the events
of Bloody Sunday,
and after the peace
thrown away,
and the guns still hidden,
and the red hand
taking the ghostly reins again,
we saw the tiny twinkled
lights of violence
from every townland.

Looked in the lamp of
one another's
eyes, felt that
animal presence
riding the
night fields again and the
encroaching loss
of control in the village
that we knew heralded
the ancient panic.

So now they were waiting
in the autumn rain,
as they used to wait,
by the crossroads,
gathered on both sides
to see what was anticipated
to be a miracle,
though at first, everyone averted
their eyes from what they
knew to be, in these times, too old
and too innocent a magic
to believe in.

The beast
somehow caught
and led between
everyone
and the man waiting
in the hushed hysteria.

His mouth moving
close to the ghost ear
they saw a hand pass over
the twitched shoulder
and felt the first
frightened shudder of the horse
pass back through the crowd
like a wave breaking.

"For Christ's sake
give him room."

Then they strained to hear
what they knew could
not be heard,
in the silence they

could only wait,
their split hypnotic faith
now joined involuntary
as they watched
the calmed violence
fall away,
caught in the animal body
of his first word.

TIENAMEN
(The Man in Front of the Tank)

On the way from Kenmare
I remember the old man
at the roadside
his casual thumb following
the lane's curve
for the length of a hillside.

Shopping bags leant
against his knees, the two circles
jutting with milk, sugar, tea,
half a loaf of oat bread
cut straight down the middle.

The one hand lifted in thanks
and the other tipped to the cap's edge
before he dropped it to the door handle
lifted his bags into the back
and took his seat in the car.

That easy lack of obligation
in the swing and pitch of the bags
hitting the back seat.
I sensed in him his far-west
inheritance passed down the long
centuries of rain and cold wind,
into his body. I felt how easily
he belonged, coming out of any
weather, rain or shine
to the stranger's hospitality.

Just after the close of the door
you could smell the cut grass
on him, the well worn wool,
and the faint breath of porter.

(My great-uncle Davy
coming in from the garden,
though never the porter,
teetotal now for fifty years)

But the familiar Sunday smell
was on me now and
I drove slowly,
matching the long ease
of the miles he'd walked
from the country shop.

At the final curve of the hill
we hit the keen wind
and wide sky above his fields,
the swaying light-swept land
a patchwork of leaning walls,
scrub, scruff and rusted gates,
and at the farm track's end
found his cottage,
the walls a cracked gray
spider's web edged by blue.

I walked in with him then for the
proffered tea. The oiled tablecloth
puddled with sugar and rimed with
cup rings. In the corner by the
cracked sink a television pulled
round on the draining board.
Above the sink a shattered
window pane, and beyond, a curlew
spiralling over the green barley.

He sat me down and set
the kettle on the blue gas flame
talked of his son
and when he might come back
to these broken walls.
"Set them straight, by God."

I thought of loneliness,
how it works at the edge
of all experience.

He filled the teapot,
set down the milk jug,
the sugar, the cups,
rattling the saucers
with a shaking hand.

About to say something
more, the name of his son
half-formed on his lips,
he stopped himself
and looking round
for a help that was not present
jabbed the television's
waiting button.

I waited one half second
for the particular
unwanted and distant
form of oblivion we were
about to join on the screen.
I preferred silence,
conversation, and the view
through the cracked window,

when suddenly the image of
a great crowd and tumult,
and in the kitchen something
ancient between us recognized
the hysteria of confrontation and
at the other end of the distant square,
an enormous emptiness.

A line of tanks was pushing
slowly into the emptiness,
as if working through a
pliant powerful barrier,
but there was only a single man
holding them back,
his silhouette leaning forward
as if bowing to the tank.

The old man's hand shook
holding the pot
and the thick black tea scalded
my outstretched hand.

My wrist came fast and involuntary
to my mouth and I bit the glowing welt
pushing my tongue against the heat.

But I couldn't take my eyes
from the man in front of the tank,
his head bowed but unmoving,
as if confronting at last,
the god hidden in the metal altar.

The old man stood stock still,
then turned, looked at me,
my scalded hand,
the screen, the young man in front
of the tank. His eyes narrowed.
His faced changed
to a helpless fury. "There's a picture
for the whole fecking century,
my son's out in the world
and God knows what he's standing
in front of now, but whatever it is,
Jesus Christ, look at these fields
he'll never come back
and why should he."

[IV]

BELONGING TO THOSE I KNOW

BRENDAN

Jupiter in the western sky
and my
son walking
with the wide arc
of the sea behind him.

Above his head
the fishing pole
bent as if to catch
the day-lit star
hovering
on the broad horizon.

The mere shape of him
in silhouette
I love so much.

The whip of his wrist
and rascal slant
of his cap

like some
hieroglyph
of love I deciphered
long ago
and read to myself
again and again.

When I first heard
him in the fluid darkness
before his birth,
calling to his mother and I
from the yet unknown
and unseen world
to which he belonged,

I could not know that
particular
slant of his
face or hand.
I could not know
how he would speak
to me.

Our love then was
for an unknown promise,

but just as strong
as if the promise was known.

May all our promises
from now
be just as strong
as they are hidden.

For no imagining could have
shaped you my boy
as I shape you now
with the eyes of a fatherly
love that must be
shaped itself by your growing.

If I was asked
what my gift had been
I should turn
to look at you.

You and your beloved
fishing pole
casting for a star.

EDWARD

Aquiline, yet youthful, resembling
still the photograph you showed me
of the father I could never meet,
I see your face now set against
the evening glow of hills.
Your lit profile to me well-loved
and familiar like each
Cumbrian crag and steep
to which I brought you that
first summer of our friendship.

I hear your laugh now in the quiet
dark of a fellside, our limbs tired
from a thousand feet of rock
and summer heat, the gold light
of fireflies haunting the trees below
and the ground's embracing
warmth like a loving dream,
no talk but the sound of our feet
on the quiet path to the valley floor.

We live in the shadow of those
memories as we sometimes live
in the shadow of those with
extraordinary gifts. Sometimes the days
are generous and miraculous in what
they can bestow and sometimes
a life must be measured
against a certain remembered epoch
when the veil between heaven and earth

was thin as gossamer and the shared
experience close to the angels,
for I felt our winged flight
above the valley floors
roped in one another's care
brought us to that earned necessity
which we look back to
and name as love, and we
know now that out of that towered
landscape of rock and cascading fell
we forged our friendship for a lifetime.

Each warm summer then for years
we'd take the long drive north
talking together, letting speech
and renewed friendship merge
the year we'd spent apart,
our voices warm and our eyes
following the sun's low track in the
evening sky, until our stories grew
darker and quieter like the evening ground,
and the shape of those hills
once more resembled the silhouette
of our familiar and imagined arrival.

Our silence in the car by then
a pure anticipation of that heaven
of grey and lichened stone to which
we drove. The dormant and sleeping
ropes of perlon coiled in the back
waiting to be unwound into the upper light
of a Cumbrian cliff face, you at one end,

me at the other, two minute
figures intent on their ascent
into the shadows formed
between the sun-lit upper
roofs of rock, ourselves exultant and
glowing in the evening light, far above
the sheepwalk of the waiting ground.

For it seems to me that always,
even under grey and solid cloud,
our stalwart and quiet resolution
on the journey up, watching the rain
on the windscreen would earn its just
reward in weekend sun, the great
amphitheaters of rock become
our silent stage, long climbs following
the evening rays step by lighted step
into the upper shadows
of the coming night. For you
and I in my memory are forever
framed in sunlight, our newly youthful
hearts full of that impossible
and vertical world we
learned to call our own.

Now, putting down the phone,
looking east through the window
over these once foreign, now
familiar, mountains toward you,
your voice receding into darkness
over six thousand miles of
land and turbulent water,

I feel you at a great
crossroads of movement, hesitant
only for a moment before
this new and unknown life
shaping before your eyes,
and I remember you intent,
eyes narrowed and searching,
watching the curve of the
cliff above you, one arm kept limp
beside your waist, saving its strength
while the other holds you balanced.

Feet barely touching rock,
the black edge of your climbing
shoes smearing across
the airy nothing of a wafer ledge,
you tiptoe across the hanging
arch and disappear from view.

I watch the rope pay out into
sunlight and wreathed mist
and see your reappearance
in the columned roofs above.

The way you loved to work
slowly up a long groove
escaping through a daylight gap
barely visible below,
while I paid out slowly
the lengths of patient rope.

I watch you now
and mark your ascent
into this other
more difficult territory,
each step your own,

but me still careful
to watch you,
and your progress,
the rope
between us
like a living bond

and you thankfully
unaware, my brother,
intent on the passage
not seeing
(in the closeness of that
living earth)
the terrors of the
height to which you step.

DOUGIE

My uncle Dougie
was killed
on Sword Beach,
the 6th of June,
nineteen hundred
and forty four.

The cadence
of the date
like a slow chant
in my father's mind
round the one
central memory.

Dougie taught
him how to swim
before he died.

There are other words
still said
in unassuming
reverence
when our heads bend
over the letters
and you remake
and relive

the familiar loss,
as if forging his absence
new again,
each phrase measured
by its careful
placement in silence.

His regiment,
The East Yorkshires
I remember since
childhood and,
your Grandma and Grandpa
didn't know for months,
and now in final silence
the bleak
unnatural
and late arriving telegram
folded
and unfolded
down fifty years.

Sometimes I know
my father is
a young boy again
and Dougie,
teaching him how to swim,
has suddenly turned away
as if in a dream
and looks toward
France.

Then he is low down
in the water
near the horrific shore
and my father's arms
so recently taught
to live in that element
are reaching
to pull him back.

But the weighted surge
of his elder
brother's
pack and rifle

pull too much
for the young boy's arms.

Now I remember
my father's repeated
weekend need
for the ice cold waters
where he taught me
how to swim
and his fatherly
satisfaction
at the slowly
growing strokes
that kept his son
above water.

I could not know what
was being given then
not knowing
how as the years pass
we must always strike
boldly to save those close to us,
hold them
above the drowning water
with our words,
so they live again,

if not the man,
then the loved
memory,

father to son,
brother to brother,
hand dipping in the water
toward shore,
saving them
now
as we could not then,
phrase by repeated phrase.

THE HAWTHORN

The crossed knot
in the hawthorn bark
and the stump
of the sawn off branch
hemmed by the roughened
trunk. In that
omniscient black eye
of witness
I see the dark no-growth
of what has passed
grown round by
what has come to pass,
looking at me
as if I could speak.

So much that was
good in her,
so much in me,
cut off now
from the future
in which we
grew together.

Now
through the window
of my new house
that hawthorn's
crooked faithful
trunk round
an old and broken
growth,

my mouth dumb

and
Dante's voice
instead of mine
from the open book

Brother, our love
has laid our wills to rest.
Making us long
only for what is ours
and by no other thirst
possessed.

Our life not lived
together
must still
live on apart,
longing only
for what is ours
alone,
each grow
round the missed branch
as best we can,
claim what is ours
separately,

though not forget
loved memories,
nor that life
still loved by memory,
nor the hurts
through which we
hesitantly
tried to learn
affection.

Our pilgrim journey
apart or together,
like
the thirst
of everything
to find its true form,
the grain of the wood
round the hatched knot
still
straightening
toward the light.

TWO STRANGERS

Two horses
on the wide brow of the hill
and a woman with dark hair
looking toward me
as if she knew me.

Strange and familiar
this silent togetherness,
walking the horses on the
tawny heath.

Until she stops,
gathers herself
on that white
litheness and rides
toward the Black Mountains
brooding in the west.

I follow her until
we slow together
on the round
knoll, the silence
between us
like a third companion,
the clouds streaming
from us in a wide sky
and the mountains
framing her face.

My fortieth year,
and I think of time stopped
and time slipping by
and all the other faces
in all the other years
still looking and still waiting.

They come to us
flowering and fading
through a thousand forms.

And they do not wait
until we are ready.

I remember
the dark rippled cobbles
in an ancient square
and that broken
beggar's mouth
moving slowly,
as if to open.

That beautiful
breathless woman in blue
turning toward me
in sunlight,

and
that daughter
on the flatbed truck
beseeching for her wounded
father.

The world is full
of strangers
who demand our love
and deserve it.

For their mouths
loving or helpless.
For their eyes,
beautiful or not,

for their hair,
raven or mouse,
and their faces,
clear or clouded
by their past,

and most of all
like this one,
for her courage

who asked me
a stranger
to join her,

two familiars
who might never
meet again

their faces
in this moment
calm and protected
from suffering,

looking from the white
manes of their
stamping horses,

pilgrims of the
timeless and untravelled,
over the wide curve
of a trembling world.

WORKING TOGETHER

We shape our self
to fit this world

and by the world
are shaped again.

The visible
and the invisible

working together
in common cause,

to produce
the miraculous.

I am thinking of the way
the intangible air

passed at speed
round a shaped wing

easily
holds our weight.

So may we, in this life
trust

to those elements
we have yet to see

or imagine,
and look for the true

shape of our own self,
by forming it well

to the great
intangibles about us.

Written for the presentation of
The Collier Trophy to The Boeing Company
marking the introduction of the new 777 passenger jet.

LOAVES AND FISHES

This is not
the age of information.

This is *not*
the age of information.

Forget the news,
and the radio,
and the blurred screen.

This is the time
of loaves
and fishes.

People are hungry,
and one good word is bread
for a thousand.

THIS POEM BELONGS TO YOU

This poem
  belongs to you
    and is already finished,

it was begun years ago
    and I put it away

knowing it would come
  into the world
    in its own time.

In fact
  you have already read it,
    and closing the pages
      of the book,

you are now
  abandoning the projects
    of the day and putting on
      your shoes and coat
        to take a walk.

It has been long years
  since you felt like this.

You have remembered
  what I remembered,
    when I first began to write.

THE SUN

This morning on the desk,
facing up,
a poem of Kavenagh's
celebrating a lost love.

"She was the sun," he said,
and now she still
lives in the fibre
of his arms,
her warmth
through all the years
folding the old man's hand
in hers
of a Sunday
Dublin morning.

Sometimes reading
Kavanagh I look out
at everything
growing so wild
and faithfully beneath
the sky
and wonder
why we are the one
terrible
part of creation
privileged
to refuse our flowering.

I know
in the text of the heart
the flower is our death
and the first opening
of the new life
we have yet to imagine,

but Kavenagh's line
reminds me
how I want to know
that sun,
and how I want to flower
and how I want to claim
my happiness
and how I want to walk
through life
amazed and inarticulate
with thanks.

And how I want to
know that warmth
through
love itself,
and
through the sun itself.

I want to know
that sun
of happiness
when I wake
and see through
my window
the morning color
on the far mountain.

I want to know
when I lean down to the lilies
by the water
and feel their small and
perfect reflection
on my face.

I want to know
that gift
when I walk
innocent through the trees
burning with life
and the green
passion
of the pasture's
first growth,

and I want to know
as lazily
as the cows
that tear at the grass
with their
soft mouths.

I want to know
what I am
and what I am
involved with by loving
this world
as I do.

And I want time
to think of all
the unlived lives:

those that fail to notice
until it is too late,

those with eyes staring
with bitterness,

and those
met on the deathbed
whose mouths are wide
with
unspoken love.

Every year
they keep me faithful
and help me
realize there is more
to lose
than I thought
and more at stake
than the mere
possibility
of a recognized
heroism.

They remind me
why
I want to be found by love,
why I want to come alive
in the holiness
of that belonging,
and like Kavanagh

I want to be courageous
in my terrors.

I want to know
in life or death
all the ways
the warmth of that
great rose fire
sun
in its heaven
has made me.

And everything
that made me
has been
a sun to my growing,
that is the article
of my faith,
even the darkness
of that soil that went
before the time of light
was another
kind of sun.

What I am
is what I have
been grown by,
the sun,
that great love,
all the many small loves
and that one love too
who waited so long
to find me and
who has always
walked by my side
folding my
remembering
hand in hers.

THE TRUELOVE

There is a faith in loving fiercely
the one who is rightfully yours,
especially if you have
waited years and especially
if part of you never believed
you could deserve this
loved and beckoning hand
held out to you this way.

I am thinking of faith now
and the testaments of loneliness
and what we feel we are
worthy of in this world.

Years ago in the Hebrides
I remember an old man
who walked every morning
on the grey stones
to the shore of baying seals,

who would press his hat
to his chest in the blustering
salt wind and say his prayer
to the turbulent Jesus
hidden in the water,

and I think of the story
of the storm and everyone
waking and seeing
the distant
yet familiar figure
far across the water
calling to them,

and how we are all
waiting for that
abrupt waking,
and that calling,
and that moment
we have to say *yes*,
except it will
not come so grandly,
so Biblically,
but more subtly
and intimately in the face
of the one you know
you have to love,

so that when
we finally step out of the boat
toward them, we find
everything holds
us, and everything confirms
our courage, and if you wanted
to drown you could,
but you don't

because finally
after all this struggle
and all these years,
you don't want to any more,
you've simply had enough
of drowning,
and you want to live and you
want to love and you will
walk across any territory
and any darkness,
however fluid and however
dangerous, to take the
one hand you know
belongs in yours.